WALKING STICKS

Published by Smart Apple Media

123 South Broad Street

Mankato, Minnesota 56001

Copyright © 1999 Smart Apple Media.

International copyright reserved in all countries.

No part of this book may be reproduced in any form

without written permission from the publisher.

Printed in the United States of America.

Photos: Dan L. Perlman (pages 7, 9-10, 17, 28);

Entomological Society of America/Ries Memorial Slide

Collection (cover, pages 2-3, 6, 12-16, 18-20, 22-24, 26);

Whitney Cranshaw (pages 8, 30); Wendy Meyer

(page 21); PhotoDisc (page 25)

Design &Production: EvansDay Design

Project management: Odyssey Books

Library of Congress Cataloging-in-Publication Data

Richardson, Adele, 1966–

Walking sticks / Adele Richardson. - 1st ed.

p. cm. - (Bugs)

Includes bibliographic references and index.

Summary: describes the habitat, life cycle, behavior,

predators, and unique characteristics of walking sticks.

ISBN 1-887068-37-6 (alk. paper)

1. Stick insects—Juvenile literature. [1. Stick insects.]

I. Title. II. Series: Bugs (Mankato, Minn.)

QL509.5R535 1998

595.7'29–dc21   98-15344

First Edition   9 8 7 6 5 4 3 2 1

WALKING STICKS

Adele D. Richardson

THE AIR SEEMED STILL AND ALMOST LIFELESS. YET THE LEAVES ON A NEARBY TREE *swayed* SLIGHTLY. SUDDENLY, A BARE TWIG *sprouted* LEGS AND REMOVED ITSELF FROM THE TREE. SOON, MORE AND MORE *TWIGS* BEGAN TO WALK AROUND

IN A **SLOW** AND PURPOSEFUL PACE.

What's going on? IF YOU'VE EVER SEEN A

TWIG START TO WALK AROUND, CHANCES

ARE YOU WITNESSED ONE OF THE

WORLD'S BEST DISGUISED INSECTS—

THE WALKING STICK.

About Walking Sticks

More than 2,000 SPECIES, or kinds, of walking sticks live all over the world. Most thrive in warm, tropical climates. A few species live in Europe and North America, but most make their homes in Asia, Africa, Australia, and Central and South America.

The scientific name for this unusual order of insects is *Phasmida,* which comes from a Latin word for "ghost." This is a

fitting name for a group of insects that look so much like sticks and twigs, many times even predators overlook them.

Hard to Find   Walking sticks really are masters of disguise. Their ability to CAMOUFLAGE, or blend in with their surroundings, allows them to hide from the keenest of eyes, especially when in their natural environment. Their long, thin bodies blend in perfectly with the stems of a plant. Even their legs and

Walking sticks spend most of their lives on trees and plants.

Big Sticks

These stick-like insects come in all sizes. The average length of walking sticks found in North America is around 2 inches (5 cm). Some of the longest have been found in Asia at over 12 inches (30.5 cm). To get an idea of just how huge a bug like that is, find a foot-long ruler and imagine that it has sprouted legs and is walking right past you. Now that's one big insect!

knee joints resemble plant parts! Usually, these stick insects wear the same brown or green colors found in nature. Some walking sticks have spots that make them look like tree bark. Others can even change color if they need to!

Walking sticks are also hard to see because most are NOCTURNAL. This means they come out at night (when a lot of their enemies are sleeping) to search for food. During the day they remain motionless on their tree or plant and often appear to be "playing dead." Many predators (and perhaps even you!) may look right at a walking stick and think it's just another twig.

At first glance, this hungry stick insect looks like a tree branch with half-eaten leaves.

Stick Food   Walking sticks are VEGETAR-IAN insects, which means they eat only plants. The leaves of the blackberry bush are one of their favorite foods. Usually, this "leaf only" diet is not a problem. But if a lot of walking sticks inhabit one area, they can DEFOLIATE, or strip the leaves from the plants and trees.

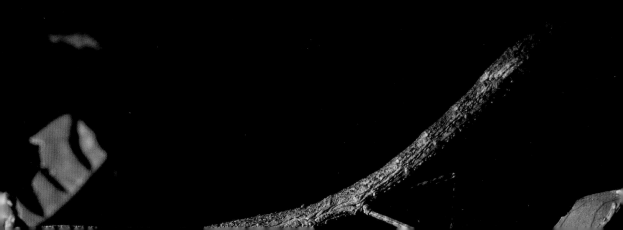

Bodies of Walking Sticks

Walking sticks may look like simple twigs, but their bodies are divided up into three sections: head, thorax, and abdomen. Like all other insects, they have six legs and breathe air.

The Head   The walking stick's antennae, eyes, and mouth are on its head. The ANTENNAE, or feelers, are usually long and very thin. They are used to feel the way ahead when this insect walks or

climbs. Male walking sticks also use their antennae to search for females.

Walking sticks have COMPOUND eyes, which means each eye has many lenses. In comparison, human eyes have only one lens. These insects can see very well and in many directions at one time.

Their powerful MANDIBLES, or jaws, are used for eating the tree and plant leaves so important to this insect's diet.

The Thorax   The THORAX is the middle section of a walking stick's body. Here is where the legs and (in some species) the wings are located.

Walking sticks move rather slowly. In

Every part of a walking stick's body is perfectly suited for its lifestyle.

fact, their legs don't allow them to jump or run. But this is no problem! Because walking sticks eat only plants, they don't have to chase after food. Some walking sticks even spend their whole lives on just one plant.

The legs of these curious creatures possess sharp little claws, which give them the ability to hang on to branches and tree bark. That's why they are more suited to climbing, which they do often.

When at rest, a walking stick holds its legs straight and stiff against its body, giving it a stick-like appearance. Sometimes

Stretching out over the tips of leaves is a comfortable way to rest for this insect.

this insect will stretch out and suspend it- self from a branch. To blend in even more, it will sway from side to side, making itself look like a twig blowing in the wind.

Flying Sticks   Most walking sticks come out only at night, but a few species are DIURNAL. That means they are active during the day. These are the winged species. Some of these flying "sticks" have surprisingly colorful HIND (rear) wings.

When at rest, the insect keeps the wings folded neatly against its body. But if threatened, it will suddenly unfold its

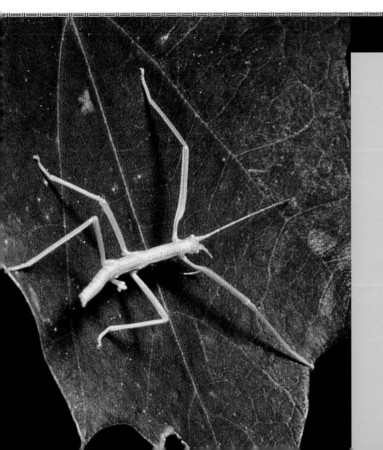

Where Did That Leg Go?

The walking stick's legs are unique because they can REGENERATE. This means the insect can grow back a leg if it loses one. Many a walking stick can also use special muscles to sever its own leg if attacked. This can leave a hungry predator with nothing but a scrawny leg while the real prize—its din-ner—gets away! The insect hobbles or moves around with only five legs until the new limb grows back. But the new leg will always be weaker than the original one.

wings and quickly show the colorful underside. This is called FLASH COLORATION and is used to startle and scare off enemies. The male Thorny Stick Insect (*Heteropteryx dilatata*) from Malaysia flashes his bright reddish wings for protection against intruders.

Even if a walking stick has wings, it

normally doesn't fly. Most of the time the wings are used as a parachute so the insect can float down to the ground in case of an emergency.

***

The Abdomen   The ABDOMEN is the third section of a walking stick's body. Here is where its respiratory system and reproductive organs are found.

A walking stick breathes air as a human does, but it doesn't take in air through its mouth. Instead, it has tiny holes along its abdomen (and some on its thorax) called SPIRACLES. The spiracles take the air into the insect's respiratory system, where the oxygen then gets delivered to the rest of the body. Because of how this insect breathes, you may see a walking stick with its head in a puddle. You can be pretty sure it hasn't drowned—it's probably just thirsty!

***

Laying Eggs   The female's abdomen is usually longer than the male's because she

The abdomen of this leaf-footed walking stick resembles a plant leaf.

This Giant walking stick is protecting itself with color.

produces the eggs, which can be rather large. She lays her eggs with an organ called an OVIPOSITOR. Some species bury their eggs with spiky tubes that grow on their abdomens. But most walking sticks simply drop their eggs to the ground. In fact, if you are in a highly populated walking stick area, the dropping of eggs can sound like rain as they fall to the forest floor.

This walking stick was once a tiny nymph only ¼ inch (6 mm) long.

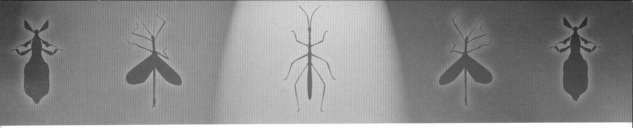

It's a Stick's Life

Most types of walking sticks live for one to two years after they hatch. The larger insects tend to have a longer life span. During the course of their lifetime, walking sticks will go through three stages of development. The stages are egg, nymph, and adult.

Eggs Walking stick eggs are usually brown and look like little seeds. Some

hatch in as little as one month, while others take over a year. Temperature and humidity play a big role in determining when the eggs hatch. They need more time in colder, drier climates.

The female lays the eggs one at a time, and over the course of her life will produce 100 to 200. She either places them in a hiding spot, usually around food, or drops them to the ground. Soon after the eggs are laid, she dies.

The young are curled up tightly inside the egg, and once hatched can be up to ¼ inch (6 mm) long. When it's time to hatch, part of the egg opens up like a door and the young walking stick backs out. Its legs are the last part of the body to come out of the egg.

This walking stick egg is magnified many times.

The Nymph Stage Newly hatched stick insects are called NYMPHS. They are perfect little copies of the adults except they don't have wings. Walking sticks do all of their growing during the nymph stage. However, their bodies don't expand as a human's does. Instead walking sticks MOLT, or shed their skin, when it becomes too small. The old skin splits and falls off to reveal a larger insect.

During these molts the young are also able to grow new body parts. This growth

A walking stick nymph must shed its skin to grow a bigger body.

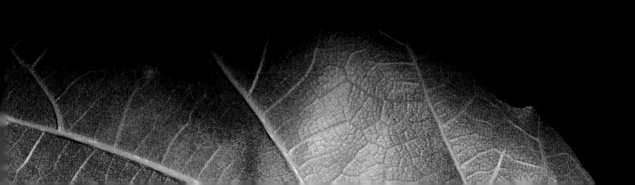

stage lasts anywhere from three to six months, depending on the species. In between these molts, the young will slowly grow wings if they are a flying species. Nymphs usually go through six or seven molts before becoming adults.

Look closely: Is this a simple twig or a stick insect?

The Adults   Once a walking stick reaches the adult stage, it is ready to look for a mate. However, in some species there are no males, and the females begin laying fertile eggs as soon as they reach adulthood. Scientists call these species PARTHENOGENETIC.

Mating

When a male is involved in mating, he is usually in danger of becoming a predator's next meal. He will grasp the female in such a way that his body often hangs out in full view from the plant he is clinging to. This makes the male an easy target. What is even more dangerous for him? Mating can last for several hours, days, or even weeks!

Scientists aren't sure why walking sticks take so much time to mate. It could be that the male wants to protect the fertile female from other males or from predators. For example, if a bird saw a pair of walking sticks mating, the obvious (and easiest) choice would be to take the male that's in full view. If this happens, the female usually survives to lay the eggs.

Leaf Insects

Leaf insects (family *Phyllium*) are a close relative of walking sticks. As their name implies, they look just like leaves. There are about 50 species of leaf insects throughout the world. They can be found in Southeast Asia, Australia, and New Guinea.

Leaf insects have flat, wide bodies, and many have patterns resembling the spots of decay sometimes found on real leaves.

A female leaf insect cannot fly because it has hard front wings. These wings even have little veins running through them that resemble the veins on leaves. A male has tiny front wings and well-developed rear wings that enable flight. Leaf insects, like most of their walking stick cousins, are nocturnal.

These insects are disguised even better than walking sticks. In fact, they look so much like leaves that members of their own species may not recognize them. A leaf insect might even chomp on another's wing, thinking it's food! Most are green, but some species have the wilted brown appearance of dead leaves.

Leaf Babies Even though the leaf insect is better disguised (and protected from predators) than a walking stick, it is not very common. For one thing, leaf insects reproduce slowly. A female lives only about three months after reaching adulthood, and in her lifetime she will lay approximately 100 eggs. Like walking sticks, some

This leaf insect looks much more like a plant than like a bug.

species have very few or no males at all.

The babies of leaf insects hatch without wings and are a reddish-brown color. After a few more weeks, they turn a yellow-green shade. The nymph stage for these "wandering leaves" lasts from two to four months. After the final molt, the nymphs become adults and begin to mate.

Looking for a mate is a tough job when you look like a plant.

Keep Away!

Many animals consider walking sticks food. Bats, birds, monkeys, and lizards are some of their most dangerous enemies (PREDATORS). These insects, fragile though they may seem, use interesting tactics that help keep them safe. You've already read about their defenses, such as camouflage, changing color, the ability to sever a leg or two, and that they are nocturnal. But what other defenses do they have?

Some of these hungry bats will snack on walking sticks after the sun sets.

Some walking sticks are able to make noise to scare off enemies. The Jungle Nymph *(Heteropteryx dilatata)*, a species from Malaysia, can make a hissing noise with its wings. Other walking sticks have tiny prickles all over their bodies, which are very sharp and can draw blood. Some species have glands on their thorax that they use to release a nasty-smelling spray.

This spray can cause eye swelling and even temporary blindness. In fact, if a tree were highly populated with walking sticks, a human couldn't stand beneath it because of the irritating chemicals! The defenses of other species include spitting or vomiting at a predator. Wouldn't that make you run the other way, too?

Something must have scared this brown stick insect (Ctenomorphodes tessularus) *for it to show its wings.*

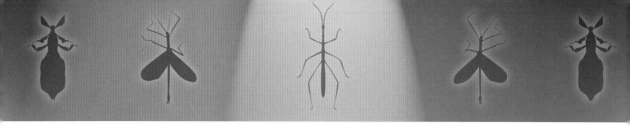

Walking Sticks as Pets

Though they are not common, walking sticks can be fun and unique pets. You can purchase walking sticks at some pet stores or through a breeder. Or, if you have a really sharp eye, you can find them in the wild. It is best to acquire a stick insect when it's still in its nymph stage and has gone through a few molts. Before you bring your walking stick home, make sure it looks healthy and has all its body parts, like legs and antennae.

Stick Houses To house your pet "stick" it is best to use a TERRARIUM (dry aquarium) with a tight-fitting mesh lid. This allows the insect to get enough air without letting it escape. Plants and twigs should be placed inside so the "stick" can climb and eat. You already know that blackberry leaves are a favorite food, but some walking sticks also eat rhododendron leaves. Check with a breeder to find out what leaves your insect likes best.

It is also important to make sure that your terrarium is not too crowded. If there isn't enough space, your insects may start fighting with each other. Walking sticks need fresh water, too. It should be placed in a very shallow container so that the insects don't accidentally drown. It's also a good idea to gently mist the plant leaves every day with a sprayer.

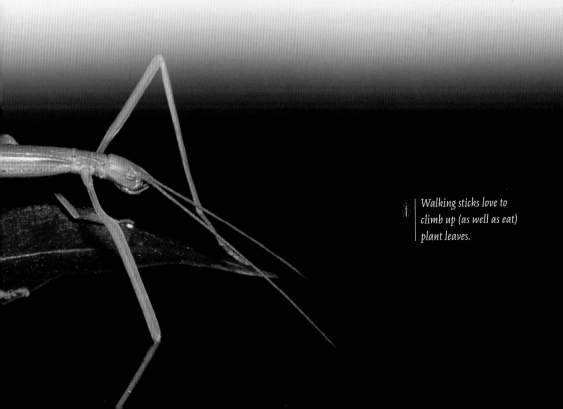

Walking sticks love to climb up (as well as eat) plant leaves.

Your walking sticks will do best in a room with a temperature between 75 and 80 degrees Fahrenheit (23 and 26 degrees Celsius). If that's not practical, you can use a lightbulb to keep the temperature constant. At night the bulb should be replaced with a red one so as not to disturb the insects. The bright light of a regular lightbulb will make them think it's still daytime, and they won't come out to feed.

You will also have to change the paper in the bottom of the cage a couple of times a week. Be careful, though, because walking sticks often drop their eggs on the ground. You wouldn't want to throw away your pet's babies!

Handling Walking Sticks   Always handle your insects with care. Remember, some walking sticks have sharp spines on their legs, or even worse, they might "lose" a leg if they feel threatened. The best way to handle a walking stick is to simply let one walk up onto your finger. If you need to pick it up, gently grasp it around the thorax.

If you're careful with your walking sticks, you may end up with a new generation every couple of years. Whether you choose to raise them, or maybe just watch them when you're outside, walking sticks are sure to keep your interest.

A pet "stick" such as this Colorado walking stick (Parabacillus coloradus), *could make you the talk of the neighborhood.*

BOOKS

How to Keep Stick Insects, Michael S. Byron, Fitzgerald Publishing, 1988

Keeping Stick Insects, Dorothy Floyd, Deanprint Ltd., 1987

A Step-by-Step Book About Stick Insects, David Alderton, T.F.H. Publications, 1992

Stick Insects, Barrie Watts, Franklin Watts, 1991

Walking Sticks, Tamara Green, Gareth Stevens Publishing, 1997

Walkingsticks, Patrick Merrick, The Child's World, 1997

CHAPTERS IN BOOKS

The Big Bug Book, Margery Facklam, Little, Brown and Company, 1994, p. 14

Bizarre Bugs, "Walking Sticks," Doug Wechsler, Cobblehill Books, 1995, pp. 5, 13

Insect, Laurence Mound, Alfred A. Knopf, 1990, pp. 8, 40, 44–45

Insect Masquerades, Hilda Simon, The Viking Press, 1968, pp. 25, 44–47, 88

Insects, Elizabeth Cooper, Steck-Vaughn Company, 1990, p. 38

Insects, "Stick-insect," Alice Fields, Franklin Watts Publishers, 1980, pp. 24, 40

FIELD GUIDES

The Common Insects of North America, Lester A. Swan and Charles S. Papp, Harper & Row, 1972

Insects of the World, Walter Linsenmaier, McGraw-Hill Book Company, 1972, pp. 74–75

The Living Community, a Venture into Ecology, S. Carl Hirsch, 1966, p. 33

WEB

"Bug Club Home Page," Amateur Entomologists Society

"Phasmatodea," Insect Compendium Index, 1997

"Phasmida Home Page," Gordon Ramel (entomologist), 1997

"Phasmids," The Phasmid Study Group, 1997

"Stick-Insect Home Page," Mark Watson (entomologist), 1997

ENCYCLOPEDIAS

Compton's Encyclopedia online

Encyclopedia of Insects and Arachnids, Maurice and Robert Burton, BPC Publishing, Ltd., 1984, pp. 179–180

The Encyclopedia of Wildlife, Castle Books, 1974, p. 44

Grzimek's Animal Life Encyclopedia, Vol. 2, Insects, 1974

Illustrated Wildlife Encyclopedia, Vol. 21, Funk & Wagnalls, 1980, pp. 2389–2391

NSA Family Encyclopedia, Vol. 17, 1992

MAGAZINE ARTICLES

"Go Wild in the Classroom," *Times Educational Supplement*, May 1996, p. XII

"Over to You," *Wild About Animals*, July 1996, p. 54

"Stick Insects," *Journal of Biological Education*, Spring 1994, p. 19

"Stick Insects Find Seedy Solution to Safeguarding Eggs," *New Scientist*, February 20, 1993, p. 16

"Twig to Stick Insects," *Australian Geographic*, Issue 47, p. 19

"When an Insect Is More Like a Plant," *Nature Australia*, Fall 1996, p. 30

"When Is a Stick Not a Stick?" *Natural History*, June 1992, p. 30

MUSEUMS

California Academy of Sciences
Golden Gate State Park
San Francisco, CA

The Milwaukee Public Museum
Milwaukee, WI

Smithsonian Institution
Washington, DC

I N D E X